The Mindful Activist Cascadia College Talk 1

Matt Ready: Thank you. That was a very nice welcome. I'm going to tell you guys a little bit of my story today, but I want to get some idea of who's in the room here. So I have two questions for you guys. We'll start with a simple one. Who here considers themselves an activist? You can raise your hand if you consider yourself an activist.

Professor: In our language it's called—remember we saw that video tape—it's not just like a non-racist, it's anti-racism, actually does something.

Matt Ready: Are you referring to -- you said racism?

Professor: Well, we saw a little clip about what's the difference between being a non and being anti, and anti is equivalent in the video to actually doing something, not just saying, "I'm not this, I'm not this."

Matt Ready: Okay. All right, so again. Hands up high if you consider yourself an activist. Give me a sense. And now, who here has a really good answer for the question, why are we here? Why are you here in this room today? Yes?

Student 1: [Unintelligible 00:02:28]

Matt Ready: Okay. Great.

Student 2: To learn something new.

Matt Ready: All right.

Student 3: To solve [unintelligible 00:02:38] bring down false [unintelligible 00:02:38] about preconceived notions that people have about certain things.

Student 4: What's that?

Matt Ready: To help bring out preconceived notions about certain things. A specific subject you're...?

Student 3: Mainly right now on the Baltics, religion and [unintelligible 00:02:56] conflicts.

Matt Ready: Nice, all right. Who else? A couple more answers. Anyone else? Why are you here? I've learned over my years, over the last 10 years, that's a really big question. You need to know why you are where you are. Why your body is where it is. If you ever become an activist or participate in activism, it's really important to know why you're standing where you're standing, 'cos sometimes you're putting yourself in harm's way, so you sort of learn, you always know why you're there, and if you don't have a reason to be somewhere, you just leave. Normally, when I talk to groups, I do it in a format called "an open space." Anyone ever participated in an open space gathering? Anyone knows what an open space is?

Student 1: No.

Matt Ready: Okay, an open space, you would get a bunch of people together like this and you would say, "Whoever wants to suggest a topic to talk about, you write it and -- say you write it up here, you may have 10 topics, and then everyone sort of gets a spot and you just go to the one you want to go to. And you don't have to stay there, you can go an listen, or you can leave it, go to another one. It's really freedom of movement, and that's what I'm most comfortable with, because it feels kind of oppressive to me to be sort of forced to sit and listen to someone for 2 hours. I never do this, and this is kind of fun, you're like a captive audience.

All right, so where to get into it? My story, my goals, my tactics, my current work, you're going to learn a lot about me today. I grew up in Maryland, obviously I'm a member of the privileged class, you know, white mainstream America. I studied Philosophy in school, this is my mom she died of cancer 10 years ago, I was a big artist in

The Mindful Activist

school. When I got into college I studied Thoreau, anyone ever read Thoreau? *Walden*? Good stuff. I love Thoreau. He's got this great attitude, very much like I said about life, you know, he's like, know what you're doing and why you're doing it. He believes in simplicity, and he believes in just sort of seeking your path, you know, not doing what everyone around you tells you to do. That's something that has been very essential to me all my life. After college, I went to a place called Twin Oaks, essentially a commune in Virginia. It's been around for like 30 or 40 years, where they try to make a truly socialist communal society. All work is equal there, it doesn't matter if it's taking care of the kids, doing dishes, making money, they just count work as an hour of labor. It's the most egalitarian place I've ever seen, but they do a lot of work there. For me it was too much, they do 40 hours of work a week and I know that sounds like mainstream, but Thoreau said you could like live off of four hours a day of work, and I was like, I like that. Four hours a day of work and then I can go and do art, and write, and explore life. Anyone like that idea? Four hours a day of work?

Students: Yes.

Matt Ready: It sounds pretty good, yeah? By the way, anytime if you want to just raise your hand and ask me a question, feel free, okay? Yes?

Student 3: You said like "egalitarian"?

Matt Ready: Egalitarian?

Student 1: What's that?

Matt Ready: It just means equal, *égal* is the root, it just means equal. As equal as possible. So right now, this is not an equal power dynamic in this room 'cos I have the power, on the speaker, I have sort of -- but if this was egalitarian, we'd have to agree who's going to speak and how are we going to decide who gets to speak. And one solution for that is like a talking stick or a talking rock. Anyone ever used that in a group? That's an egalitarian solution, unless you start fighting over the rock or the stick. That's a power struggle.

Okay, so I moved to Port Townsend Washington. Anyone ever been there? No? It's a cool little town, cool community. I was just going to live a simple life through art, get whatever job, you know, that could make me enough money to live and just sort of -- I was enjoying my life there. Y2K happened—that was the year 2000 computer glitch thing—at the same time, I was getting into the big internet explosion and started getting really fired up about the potential of the internet to change the world. I did some movie making, and actually I became a mini-activist with Y2K, trying to get the community prepared for -- some people were worried that the power grid was going to collapse due to computer malfunctions. Anyone ever hear that during the Y2K? Yeah. So, I researched and thought, you know, there is a chance there could be some bad stuff happening, so I did some Y2K activism, and that actually took me into a career at this hospital, Jefferson Healthcare, public hospital, and then I also got married and adopted five kids.

Students: [Indistinct chatter]

Matt Ready: Yeah. So one of my first attempts to change the world was called The Wisdom Project, this idea again inspired by the internet, how to extract the wisdom from masses of people, 'cos I thought that's what we all needed, wisdom, and that was fun, it sort of lasted a while and then it sort of went away. Another thing I tried was called Vaestro [as heard 00:09:01], and it was about trying again to do something with masses of people, but this time using their voices, sort of a voice blog platform, using your iPhones. You could go and ask a question and people could answer the questions, you could grade the answers, and then the best questions would bubble up to the top, sort of like -- it sort of works on [unintelligible 00:09:21] forms, Reddit, people use Reddit in here? Raise your hand if you used Reddit before. Digg? Anyone knows what Digg is? It's an old one, back in the internet early years. Okay, so Vaestro failed, that marriage ended, met a new awesome lady named Stacy and my life hit a crisis point where I was, what the heck am I doing with my life? And I turned to meditation, it's a practice that I've used throughout my life, and it's always been sort of a rock, a practice to go back to, to help me figure out where I am. Who here has ever meditated? So for those of you who don't know or never done it, meditation basically just means you stop and you be still. It creates awkwardness, I mean in a group like this, it creates awkward silence, but it also creates awkward silence when you're by yourself, so you're just sitting there, the only thing making noise is that voice in your head, and then you have to just listen to it, or decide what you're going to do with it. It's very powerful to sit for any amount -- 10 minutes, it's powerful, if you've never done it before, just sitting still. Yeah?

Student 5: Can you do it like [unintelligible 00:10:41]?

Matt Ready: Yeah. If you want to try meditation, I'm actually putting out a book about it, but it's basically just sitting still. There's lots of different styles, and do it five minutes in the morning and see what it does. If you really want to get a taste of it, 20 minutes is the way to go, 20 minutes in the morning. Yeah?

Student 2: Do you need specific meditation or is it just like you said, general meditation, being quiet, thinking?

Matt Ready: The practice -- well, meditation is like dancing, and so in dancing there's very structured forms and there's very loose forms, you know, where you do whatever you want. I prefer the loose forms of meditation where you can do whatever you want, but there's a lot to learn from being completely still, 'cos you can kind of like entertain yourself, if you start walking, distracting yourself it gives you something -- it might let you ignore some of the things your mind is telling you to listen to. So it's definitely, it's good exercise to be completely still. And then another practice that I really respect is journaling after you meditate. You journal 10 minutes, then just writing, or meditate 10 minutes, then journal and just write down whatever you remember from your meditation sit. That's what I'd recommend, and then you could journal about [unintelligible 00:12:04] too. Anyways, I could talk for two hours about meditation, but that's not what we're going to do today. One thing that happened when I was meditating was the Occupy movement, the U.S. Occupy Wall Street movement was exploding. Anyone heard of that? Raise your hand if you heard about Occupy. Some of you have not heard of it. It's a fascinating world. Occupy was a global movement that erupted in the U.S. at Zuccotti Park in 2011, Zuccotti Park in New York. It was actually inspired by the Arab Spring. Who here's ever heard of the Arab Spring? So, there's lots of interesting stuff you're going to learn today, it's interesting to me, which is good since I'm the speaker. Occupy was sweeping the U.S. and people activists were coming out of the woodworks, and they were talking about the 99%, how 1% of people in this country own like, it's something like 90% of the wealth in this country. You guys have heard that before? Aware of that? It's a massive imbalance of wealth distribution in our country. On top of that, money controls our democracy. Anyone disagrees with that, that money controls, decides who gets elected, decides our elections? If anyone wants to challenge me, I'd love to argue with you. Okay.

Student 1: May be later.

Matt Ready: Okay.

Student 2: It's a tough argument.

Student 3: Yea.

Matt Ready: [Laughs] So people were coming, and I was sick and frustrated with this myself, but I didn't think anyone else cared, so when people started taking to the streets and did exactly what they were saying, this was the critic they were saying, money is controlling our country, very much like Bernie Sanders. Bernie Sanders --

Student 1: Bernie is the man.

Student 2: Where did he go?

The Mindful Activist

Matt Ready: Occupy paved the way in this country for Bernie Sanders to be able to talk what he talked. He was talking the language that the Occupy movement brought into the mainstream. So I was inspired by this, and I was like, I want to get involved with Occupy, so I went to Seattle and found the Occupy Seattle group, went to one of their general assemblies, talked to people, helping to organize it, and I decided –I had to decide either if I wanted to help organize, or join Occupy Seattle or go somewhere, or try to do something in Port Townsend where I lived. So this was a tactical decision, and that's what all of activism is. If you want something to change, you're always making decisions in what action you take. And so that was the first action tactical decision of my activist journey, and I chose to focus on Port Townsend and try to get things going there. I learned alot about egalitarian facilitation, which again it's about how do you work with a group and have completely equal power, 'cos most groups, most ways societies around the world work is they create hierarchy. That's just the easiest, simplest way to make the group function: create a hierarchy, say someone is the leader. But that's another massive innovation in the Occupy movement, 'cos it was trying to be egalitarian, it was trying to be a leaderless movement, which required really skilled facilitation, and I'm a group facilitator, so I studied that and learned how to do it. So I just walked up to the Occupy Port Townsend group, it was just sort of a Sunday two-hour protest, and I just said, "Hey guys, do you want to do something bigger? Do you want to maybe get a general assembly going? A bigger -- and sort of expand our numbers and see if we could do stuff? People were receptive and we got things going. And a lot of things happened. We had a massive, and I probably should share some pictures of it later -- this is a picture of the first Occupy Port Townsend General Assembly. It's one of the oldest -- it is the oldest county in Washington State, so it's an interesting demographic of people to try to stir up and to try to mobilize. But things happened, we had a lot of -- let me see if we have some pictures -- this is me, we did a lot of Bank of America protests, 'cos Bank of America was kind of a symbol or corporate power. Yes?

Student 3: I was actually doing a project on [unintelligible 00:16:49] to like problems, and I was wondering if what we have is like solutions for like solving the problem?

Matt Ready: Solutions, let's comment on that.

Student 2: I'm also going to follow up on that question too.

Matt Ready: Yeah.

Student 2: But later on, I want to see if you mention it.

Matt Ready: Sure. We will get to my ideas for solutions. So this was at Bank of America, this was me going to the Occupy National Gathering in Philadelphia, marching with some pretty crazy activist, amazing activists there. This was from the day that we basically shut down Bank of America, we did a march and set this giant tent right in front of the front door so people couldn't really get in, then people went around and blocked the drive-through, and that's me sitting in the tent with a couple of my friends, all activists. This is people laying down at the drive-through, that's me. We had music blasting, they put caution tape to block the driveway. We fully expected to get arrested that day, so we were just sitting there waiting, but the police came, and they were very liberal police force and they decided, go ahead, shut down for the day, and they didn't arrest anybody. We were all kind of shocked, but stirred people up. Bank of America then hired two full-time security guards, so we considered we did some economic improvement in the town, we created two full-time jobs, security guards. This is also the Occupy National Gathering, and this is me right there, sitting there, and this was chaos, there was not good facilitation, and this was a group surrounded by militarized police and park police. I ended up facilitating at the third Occupy National Gathering, participated in tons of marches, witnessed many interesting police confrontations, witnessed violence, and I had many of these -- my goal by going to these big gatherings was trying to network, trying to figure out how this National Occupy movement could make a difference, could actually solve some of these problems. And so I wanted to talk about tactics, I wanted to talk

The Mindful Activist

about what are we doing, why are we doing it, how are we doing it, and there were other people that wanted to, but not a lot. Looking back, maybe I didn't try hard enough, maybe I should have pushed harder. I think I was personally always afraid of sort of stepping up to be in a leader-ish position, and when you're in the Occupy movement it was really apparent, especially when you went to the National Gatherings, it was a group very sensitive to power and to privilege, and to whether -- it's all white male, I was in a tricky spot, and I did not want to be part of the problem, and so it held me back some. This is me facilitating at the Occupy, third Occupy, this is a gathering in Olympia, interesting Occupy event, that's when we occupied the Courthouse in Port Townsend, we did that one night.

Okay. So the Occupy movement stops, it basically stops because the police raided all the Occupy camps and shut it down. And then, for whatever reason it sort of fizzles and evolves -- I think what basically happened is people started going into politics, being candidates and spreading in different ways. I don't know, that's another topic. So I got to go back to my life, like that was a great burst of activism, and I sort of go back to living my life, I'm working at the hospital this whole time, and then a good friend who has a very incredibly painful medical condition, I'm seeing my friend suffering and I'm saying, you knock, I work at the hospital, why don't you go to the hospital? Why don't you go to the doctor? She says, no, because she's sick of paying off medical bills. She doesn't want to go because she knows they're going to want an MRI or something and it's going to cost $2,000, she's going to owe at least $1,000 of that, and she's just sick of it so she'd just rather suffer. And so I'm just watching my friend basically cry in pain, she's suffering so much and again I go into problem-solving mode, what do I do? I want to solve this problem. And I struggle right there, you know, I go to the hospital, I talk to different departments, I try to see what they can do for her, there's no real solution, healthcare -- this opened my eyes to how big of a mess healthcare is in this country. We have the most dysfunctional healthcare system in industrialized nations in the world, because we have this octopus of a multi payer healthcare system, as opposed to a universal healthcare system like smart countries have.

So I started thinking about this, so my activist sort of energy started thinking about this in healthcare and in my workplace. I think it's absurd that this hospital where I've worked at for like 14 years is not caring for people in our community that need it, and I'm like, there has to be -- you know we don't have universal healthcare in this country, maybe we could do something in our county, just to at least make sure people in our county can get care. It doesn't sound like that difficult a problem, right? I'm like, fine, let the rest of the country suffer, but let's do something in our city or our county. So I started doing research, what are other cities, counties and hospital districts in the country doing? I figured, I can't be the first one that looked at suffering in a community healthcare and just said, we could actually solve this on a local scale, and I was right. There were other places that tried to do this. The most impressive one was San Francisco. It did something called Healthy San Francisco, and that was basically one leader, Gavin Newsom, who was Mayor at the time of San Francisco. He got elected and he said, "Let's solve healthcare for the people of San Francisco," and when he got into office he just said to his minions, "Gather leaders of hospitals and of city governments, business leaders, all the power people in the city, create a committee and their task is to come up with a solution so that everyone in San Francisco can get healthcare," and he gave them like three months to work on it. He didn't have to have the solution, he just had to say, this is the problem. You state the problem and you say, let's solve it, and you say, try, try to solve it. And they came up with this Healthy San Francisco program, and it worked really well. I actually have a friend living in San Francisco who said he [unintelligible 00:24:44] incredibly. Gavin Newsom is a kind of a very cool—can I swear in here?—he's sort of a badass in terms of like politicians. He was also the guy that kind of really kick-started the same-sex marriage sort of revolution that sort of swept the country. Many years ago he one day said, "You know what? We're just going to start accepting gay marriage certificates in San Francisco," and it was absolutely cutting edge and blew up across the country. A lot of same-sex marriage activists actually thought it was a bad idea, they didn't think our country was ready for it, but you know, it's like pushing the envelope in different areas sort of helps stir up the energy in other people.

So anyway, back to what the heck I was going to do for my friend in my county. How could I make this happen? And again, I was sitting there like, what could I do? Any ideas? I was working at the hospital and studied this. Anyone guess what I did? Or any even things they considered? Yes?

Student 2: Did you try talking to different people at the hospital?

Matt Ready: Good! Talking to people in the hospital. Any other ideas of what I could try?

Student 1: Fundraiser.

Matt Ready: Fundraiser, try to just make money to help pay for -- create a fund or something?

Student 1: Yeah.

Matt Ready: Good! Any other ideas?

Student 3: Petition.

Matt Ready: Petition? Yeah. Who would I be petitioning?

Student 3: The Mayor and probably scoping his office, county, court.

Matt Ready: Yeah. See, and that's a big decision, you know, if I'm going for the county, there's a county commissioners. So what I did, one I started to believe that the hospital district, I believe they had enough resources to do this, and so I was focusing there. Then I ended thinking about who's in power in the hospital, who controls the hospital district? And in all my years working at the hospital, I believed it was the CEO, the CEO was really the one that was making all the decisions for how the hospital worked. That's always the way I thought about it. I knew there was a Board of Commissioners that had some role in the hospital, but we never really saw them, never really talked to them, but as I thought about it

I realized there is an interesting question there, who do you talk to, the CEO or the Board? So what I did from my job, and that was pretty high-up in the organization in what's called the Performance Improvement Office, I mean I worked with all the directors, the CEO and Strategic Leadership Group, which is like the officers, all the time. I just started sharing my ideas, what if we did something like Healthy San Francisco? We could do it this way. I just started suggesting it and talking about it, and I started to feel resistance. I started to feel people -- I felt some people excited about the idea, but I could feel the institutional resistance to my ideas. So I pushed on that a little bit, but I was like, this is not fast enough. I may have made a little progress but this is nowhere near fast.

Basically, after thinking about it, I was decided the commission was the way to go, 'cos they were the ultimate authority in the district. And even if I convinced the CEO to go full on with what I was thinking, if the Commission wasn't on board, then he would have a problem. So I was like, the Commission is the way to go, the authorities of the hospital district, just like Gavin Newsom down in San Francisco, the ones in charge need to be saying, this is what we need do, we want to achieve. And so I was like, how do I get the Commission to own this? To do this? And to champion this? And these were the -- I could've asked you guys what you think the possibilities are, but this is what I came up with. I could find someone to run, to be a candidate and try to help them win and help them change the priorities of the Commission, or I could do something really crazy, which would be the candidate myself and run for the Commission. The only problem is if I won, I couldn't work at the hospital, and the Hospital Commissioner makes only about $10,000 a year and I was making about $50,000 a year, and I was working only 30 hours a week. Thoreau would have been thrilled, he would have been like, "You're doing pretty well," making good money, working less than the 40 hours a week that Twin Oaks would've made me do. So it was a very difficult point in my life, a very big decision point, like this again is where meditation comes in.

So I decided to run for office, and that guy is my Campaign Manager, that guy I'm holding there. He was also an activist with

The Mindful Activist

me, but he also was a -- he ran for office himself before Occupy. So I transformed myself into politician Matt, and that's my campaign photo and I decided to run. I'm just deciding whether or not to show you any of these videos. All right, we'll see if it works, at least you need to know that, let's see what happens with that video link.

Student 1: Everything explodes.

Matt Ready: Everything will explode? All right. [Video playing] That's enough of that. So I'd already announced that I was a candidate, but this was the first time I went into the board room and spoke publicly and said, this is what I think we should do, what I think the hospital should do. I guarantee you this was terrifying, going in there and doing this. I mean I'd worked at the hospital, and it was a high pressure situation. And also, I bit the bullet and I brought in the video camera and videotaped it, so I knew I was going to use it on my campaign website. So then I was also interviewed by the local paper.

[Video plays]

Interviewer: So was it a surprise that you decided to run for the Hospital Office, was it something, a decision that you'd been making for a long time?

Matt Ready: I think about a year ago I decided -- I first had the realization that this was the real possibility, and then I think it was about three months ago it was definite that I was going to run. There were a number of different things I could have tried to try to make some changes, so I was exploring different options, talking to other people...

[End of video]

Matt Ready: All right, so I'm about to say what I already said to you guys, why I decided to run, because that was the only way to make change. So once you run for office, your life transforms. I don't consider it an enjoyable experience, you know, to have all that attention, the articles written about you, to have letters to the editor written about you, there's negative stuff, it's not really fun, but I believed in what I was doing and I had really important support, I had supportive people around me, you don't run for office alone, and in fact, I don't think you really do anything significant, activist-wise, alone. You want to have a network of support, so if you have like an idea of something that you want to do, first step is find four or five other people that also want to do something about that, 'cos you need that kind of support; one, to help you think through what you're doing, and also just that support when things go rough.

So another thing I had to do was choose who I was going to run against. There were two people up for election, and so I had control of when I said which opponent I was choosing, I had declared I was running but I didn't say who I was running against. Everyone wanted to know, my opponents wanted to know, but that was one of the few things I had control over. I didn't have to tell them until I registered, so I didn't tell anybody. I let these people sitting on the board sweat until the last minute, and I decided to run against the President or the board, who was a retired MD, and very right-winged politically, a very right-winged politician. So then we had the whole campaign, with debates, speeches, door knocking, fund raising, pain, awkwardness, we had some of my old writings come to light during the campaign, I had a lot of pretty free willing, activist things written on this blog, one of which was that corporations are evil "f-ing" monsters. So that came out a few weeks before election day, but you know, you just bite the bullet and you speak honestly. The reason I did, when the journalist asked me about that, I said, "I shouldn't have called them evil monsters," she was nice enough to leave out that I'd called them evil "f-ing" monsters, she just said I'd called them evil monsters, and I said I should have called them sociopathic monsters, 'cos they're not necessarily evil, they're just corporations that are just sociopaths. They just care about money, they care nothing about emotions or humanity. They are abstract entities we create for a purpose, but do not have a heart or a soul. So they are sociopaths and we should treat them like sociopathic robots and not like human beings, so that we can control them. Anyways, that got in, my response got into the article and I didn't know if that had blown the whole election for me, but it did not. I won.

Students: Oh! Good.

Matt Ready: I won, yeah. And this is another thing I did during the campaign. I met with Sherry Appleton, she's a Washington State Representative 'cos she is the sponsor of a single-payer healthcare bill for Washington State, and so I called her up and said, "I'm running, I'm going to be totally talking about your bill." She met with me and she endorsed me and so I was the first -- I bet I was the first public hospital district candidate to get endorsed by a State Representative so blatantly. That was pretty cool. So I won. I won by 200 votes. I immediately resigned from my job and I started learning everything I can about how the heck to do this Public Hospital Commissioner thing and try to actually now make a change, 'cos now I'm 20% of the powers of the Board. There's five hospital commissioners and I'm only one vote, and they all campaigned against me, they hate me. I mean, they did, they really -- I mean I could feel the hostility when I joined that Commission. Probably I don't want to say it that way, I'm videotaping this, maybe I'll cut that little piece out.

Students: [Laughter]

Matt Ready: They welcomed me on to the Commission and it was a great experience. And it was really fascinating learning about how that power really works. Now we're going on to me as activist politician, and I had two goals: single-payer healthcare, pushed from the Commission level, and try to solve the access to healthcare problem. I had to figure out how to do that, especially with not having the majority power on the Board.

It's been a long story, I'm going to tell you about a few of the interesting moments where I really had to make some big decisions of what tactics to take. The first one was that we would sit in the board room and—this goes back to the egalitarian facilitation thing, where it's really important to decide who gets to speak and how long they get to speak. That's how -- that's power, you know. Verbal space, and I'm taking up all this verbal space in this room right now talking so much, but the verbal space in the room is a resource that we are -- and anytime you enter a room you are agreeing how you are going to share that resource. That's why it's really important for me to say, raise your hand if you want to talk, 'cos I'm not going to sit here just like, talk down to your throats. But in a board room, or in a legislature, it gets really important, who controls who speaks. So we get in there and I want to talk about some stuff, so I raise my hand. They weren't even raising their hand, they were sort of like talking, and I was like being polite and raising my hand and I would speak, but the Chair would cut me off, and just be like, we don't have time man, and just try to move on. And it was very aggressive and people came up to me after the meeting and they were like, that was really, I mean, they found it uncomfortably rude the way they were trying to just keep me from even talking. And so I had to think, okay, how am I going to deal with this? What tactic do I use? Any ideas? What do you do if you're in a --?

Student 3: Aggressively assert yourself.

Matt Ready: What?

Student 3: Aggressively assert yourself.

Matt Ready: Aggressively assert, I could do that, I could raise my voice, yeah?

Student 4: Bring outside resources.

Matt Ready: Outside resources? Who, I mean, police? I don't know, security guard?

Student 5: Blackmail.

Matt Ready: [Laughs] What?

Student 5: Blackmail.

The Mindful Activist

[Laughter]

Matt Ready: I'm not even going to respond to that one.

[Laughter]

Student 6: You could use evidence to support your case sort of to say you're making [unintelligible 00:40:24] facts, kind of hard to deny that.

Matt Ready: You would think so, but if they don't even let you speak your evidence, then you're kind of in a bind there. It's a really tricky situation, so the first thing I did was I asked, what are the rules of this room? Do you have any rules? Or is this literally just a slug fest of who speaks the loudest and longest? And the truth is they didn't really have -- they said they followed *Robert's Rules*. Who's heard of *Robert's Rules*? No one? *Robert's Rules* is basically the way every political body in this country works. It's the old, you know, there's someone that's the Chair of the room, the Chair recognizes people, and then you can make a motion, and a motion has to be seconded.

Students: Oh.

Matt Ready: Yeah, that's *Robert's Rules*. That's all *Robert's Rules*, created by this guy named?

Students: Robert.

Matt Ready: Robert, that's right. So they said they were following *Robert's Rules* in theory, but they weren't actually following them, but because they said they were, I could just refer to that. I guess I did what you said, who said outside authority? Yeah. So that's what I did. The outside authority was the rules they said they were using, and I tried to use that, but they still were -- the Chair just has a lot of power in *Robert's Rule*, so they can cut you off. And the other thing they can do is just ignore your suggestion. Like I can make a motion, and they could just -- no one seconds it, no one talks about it, and so

The Mindful Activist

I'm really dead in the water there. So I was like, I don't want to sit on this Board for six years and just be walked over and not have any of my motions even considered or discussed. So the tactic I came up with was, I'm going to record every meeting and share the audio on my website and I'm going to write up transcripts of any interesting exchanges, 'cos I want the public to know what I'm doing. I mean, they wanted to sit there and ignore everything I said and use what I consider really weak arguments against me when they did respond. I'm going to at least let everyone that voted for me and everyone in my county know exactly what's happening. And I was like, I could do that for six years. That would be fine, because that's all I had power over, I just wanted the people to know what I was trying to do and see if maybe that would stir things up. It would create openings. And these are public meetings, so anyone can record a public meeting in Washington State, you can walk in with a video camera -- oh, I forgot to ask that. Anyone that asks a question and you don't want your voice on there, if you could just tell me that and I'll edit your voice out of the video. You can tell me now or you can tell me after. Anyone has any concerns about me recording? Okay.

So, in a public meeting, anyone can record the meeting, so that was what I decided to do. So I emailed all the commissioners and said, "Heads up, I'm going to start recording the meetings and sharing the audio." That turned into a massive, massive conflict. Probably the biggest most intense conflict that I've ever been a part of for an extended period of time. But as you can see from the end here, in the end, really no one had any objection that actually held enough weight to stop the recording. It came out with a lot of different arguments to say it was different for a Hospital Commissioner to record. They tried to say because I was a commissioner, if I was recording it was now an act of the hospital and the Board has to decide if they're recording, so can't record it because I am a commissioner. I said, "I disagree," and they said, "Well, we have a lawyer that says we're right," and I said, "I don't care." And I kept recording. That's basically the story, but it was much more long and painful than that.

So this is actually recently. This is a video recording of the first meeting, or an audio recording of the first meeting where I recorded a sort of long discussion here, but we had a -- this is one recently where I pulled out my recorder and I'm going to just let you hear a little bit of what happened.

[Video plays]

Commissioner Deleo: We're not going to record this meeting, Matt.

Matt: I'm recording.

Commissioner Deleo: No, you're not.

Commissioner Dressler: That's not our policy, is it?

Commissioner Kolff: Wait, is this an official meeting?

Commissioner Dressler: It's an Official Board Meeting, but our policy states that we record when we're in our normal board situation, board meeting room at the hospital.

Commissioner Kolff: There's nothing that prohibits Matt from recording it.

Commissioner Deleo: Yes there is. It makes it official record.

Commissioner Kolff: There should be an official record if it's an official meeting.

CEO Glenn: Well, there is a legal opinion that recommends to not do this actually, but we talked about that. And you're right.

Commissioner Kolff: I guess that's before my times.

CEO Glenn: Yeah. [Crosstalk] not being difficult.

Commissioner Deleo: Are you still recording?

Matt: I'm recording the meeting.

Commissioner Deleo: See you guys later!

Matt Ready: He walked out of the room.

Student 7: Did he come back?

Matt Ready: Eventually.

Commissioner Deleo: Let me know if he turns it off.

Commissioner Buhler: This is a little counterproductive. Do you really want to do this Matt?

Matt: [Breathes deeply]

Matt Ready: That's me breathing, that's meditating in a board room. Hold on, you should hear this. This is me like stretching the silence in the board room. They're all waiting obviously. My stress level is off the charts.

Commissioner Buhler: Yes? No?

Matt: Sorry, my stress level is very high right now, so it's hard for me to speak. [Crosstalk] I did not expect a massive conflict over this. I didn't think you guys would be surprised. I recorded last year's meeting if you recall, so I've told you before, I cannot actually remember everything that is said at these meetings, and it's important to me that we take what we say here seriously and we're held accountable for what we say here. And the only way to do that, is to have an accurate record of these meetings, and so I record the meetings.

[End of video]

The Mindful Activist

Matt Ready: And then they went on there 10 minutes of coming up with reasons to try to stop me. Eventually they stopped the meeting, we just didn't have a meeting at all.

Student 1: So I find it very interesting that, I don't know who the person is, but the lady who said it was counterproductive, but the fact was that discussing this whole matter of you recording when you've already done it before was actually more counterproductive than what could've gone on -- 'cos I'm assuming you guys don't talk about just recordings at the Hospital Commission, it's like you're supposed to talk about other things.

Matt Ready: Yeah. We have other topics to talk about [laughs].

Student 1: Okay [laughs].

Student 2: I just have a question. So are there meetings annually or are they...?

Matt Ready: Twice a month

Student 2: Twice a month.

Matt Ready: Twice a month meetings.

Student 2: I would have walked out.

Matt Ready: Cool.

Student 7: I just think it's very interesting they're so worked up over it, I mean, do you really have so much to worry about that you can't be open with who you're making decisions for in the first place? Like, why can't -- if you don't feel bad about it and you feel like you're doing the right thing, why are you so upset that the people you're affecting know what you're doing? I find that really weird.

Matt Ready: Yeah.

The Mindful Activist

Student 2: They're more worried about what they're going to say than actually doing something.

Student 7: If you don't feel guilty, what's the problem?

Matt Ready: I'm with you [laughs].

Student 8: I know, because I used to be a reporter for [unintelligible 00:49:48] education, that you're supposed to have some kind of recording for every word [unintelligible 00:49:53].

Matt Ready: Well, it's not legally required at public hospital districts, but so we weren't breaking the law. That would have been easy.

Student 2: It's optional.

Matt Ready: It's optional . Yes.

Student 3: I'm wondering like, why do they're like argue, is it so much because of like money or is it just like [unintelligible 00:50:09]?

Student 2: Actually, they just don't want to be accountable for what they say.

Matt Ready: It's a good question, why -- and there's four of them, so they're -- yes?

Professor: What would you want us to know, to learn about your experience considering that we are, some of us, not activists at all? Some who are thinking about becoming activists. How can -- what could you clarify for me? What could I take away from the experience that you talked about?

Matt Ready: Sure. I think basically just, I mean, one, being an activist just means you're trying to change something. You're just actively trying to change something in the world. And so I'm basically, I'm just sort of sharing my journey through times I wanted to change everything and it's basically a journey of choosing tactics. It's always choosing actions. Whether or not it's activism in a political sense or in your life, you're always choosing tactics. So I just sort of wanted people to get a taste of these moments when I had to make a decision of what to do, and show there's different ways you can make those decisions: one, like in the board room there, you have to make the decision on the spot. Pressure's there and you have to decide right there, high pressured, and I use meditation a lot to sort of like pause things, try to stretch out the amount of time you get to think what to do. And then there's decisions that are, that you have more time, where you could sort of brainstorm different actions. And as we get to the end we'll go to my actual solution. All right.

Professor : Can I just ask the class? Are you starting to -- I mean I'm -- I think it's fascinating, I'm on three pages of taking notes. Have you come up with ideas to help you with your own project? Or...

Student 7: Yes.

Professor: Oh, great.

Matt Ready: All right. Okay, so more little activist tactical decision making that I had to do. I'll just take you through this. I want Washington State to really get behind single-payer healthcare, so how do I do that from the Commission level? It has the state level bill that's under consideration, I thought well, to start with I could get the Board to discuss it, so my first tactic was just ask them to discuss it, like, "Hey, there is a big single-payer bill, are we willing to talk about it?" They agreed and it helped that the meetings were being recorded. If I wasn't recording the meetings, it would be very easy for them to say, you know, to dismiss it, but when you're being recorded, it puts pressure on you to say something that you can defend later and then you look a little bit better to the public. And so it brought some of the better selves out of my fellow commissioners.

So they agreed to discuss it, I said if we decide we're for or against it, we should say so, and they agreed to that, and then they agreed to

The Mindful Activist

schedule a meeting to discuss single-payer, a future meeting, and so then I decided to try to raise the energy of that meeting that I put the word out to activists that this was happening. I also was the one that organized the presentations, and we had a big meeting, a lot of people from the public and we ended up being the first public hospital district to pass a resolution in favor of single-payer healthcare. That was pretty cool. Also, as a part of this, these are two experts that I networked with to bring in, and this is Steve Tharinger -- anyone knows who Steve Tharinger is? State Representative like Sherry Appleton, or other. That's me sitting on a panel at the local Unitarian Fellowship talking about single-payer, it's a week before that big board meeting. So that's one thing, a little bit of progress.

Then my next tactic, again just trying to get universal healthcare in our state, was trying to get all public hospital districts to endorse it like this public hospital district did. And so, how to do that? I decided I'm going to try to network with the commissioners, you know, again, 'cos when I go to these conferences and all the public hospital commissioners are there, I was a very small lonely voice in trying to talk about single-payer healthcare, and so I had to, like I said, build your strength in numbers. So I networked for allies and I've been doing that for about two and a half years, and we're up to about 20 public hospital commissioners that really want to get this talked about, and we're putting pressure on the Washington State Hospital Association, which has huge power for organization, and the Association of Washington Public Hospital Districts, just try to get them to start discussing it, but they're currently saying no basically. They're refusing to discuss single-payer healthcare, and so now again we're sort of blocked, so again we have to decide what to do. So, any ideas? So imagine you're a big organization and it's a club [unintelligible 00:56:21] club and you want them to -- you want them to actually support the issue, but to get them to support it, you want them to first talk about it, and they're refusing to talk about it. What do you do?

Student 2: Keep calm.

Matt Ready: Okay.

The Mindful Activist

Student 6: Or you can possibly plant a seed into those groups and then have them discuss it that way by, you know, bringing up like incentive [unintelligible 00:56:55] discuss it.

Matt Ready: Sure, so plant seeds in the people, try to get -- okay, good.

Student 1: Maybe since you have other boards to work with, maybe form a kind of leader or each board and then -- it's like a meeting within a meeting basically, the sense you're getting consensus of, okay, would you guys be willing to bring this up in your commission?

Matt Ready: Good, and that's actually what we're starting to do now, so we've got two other public hospital district boards have passed, they're not quite resolution in favor of single-payer but they're in favor of asking this organization to discuss it at our big conferences. Is there another suggestion?

Student 4: I just find it interesting how you use like transparency basically like they want to like shun that topic so [unintelligible 00:57:35].

Matt Ready: Excellent, yeah. And right now I'm telling you guys in recording this I'm going very transparent about [unintelligible 00:57:45] resisting talking about single-payer healthcare. Yeah, transparency is amazing. Sunlight is a disinfectant. Anywhere that BS is happening, just shine some light on it, it makes everyone behave a little better and it creates a, what I call, a thread of truth. A video record or an audio record of what happened is usually a thread of truth that gives you strength as long as you are being honest about what happened, and what you' re talking about, what you said and what you believe, and it gives you something to fall back on if other people are inconsistent, or they are changing their mind, or they're just using really really bad arguments. Transparency is a really powerful thing.

Student 2: With these tactics, did you find that the board was overtime more consistent or more inconsistent?

Matt Ready: The recording helped them be more consistent, and elevated the level of the conversation in the room. So at the conferences, part of networking was just getting up out of my seat and walking around every table and just walking up to the table and saying, "Is anyone here a Public Hospital Commissioner?" I would ignore everyone else at the table, and whoever said they were I would just look at them and say, "Do you support single-payer healthcare? And they would tell me yes or no. If they said yes, I'm like, "Would you want to talk about it sometime?" And they'd said yes or no. If they said yes, I wrote it down, moved on and set up a meeting. Really uncomfortable for me, I'm an introvert, I don't like going up to people and talking to them, but you know, you do what - - you do the tactic that has the most possibility for success, not the tactic that feels good. There's often the awkward uncomfortable tactics that have the most results. That's pretty much true about everything in life. Just a life tip. And I also tried to go to a board meeting of the AWPHD, I just went to it and just walked in the room, they were starting to get set up and the Director of the AWPHD campaign said, "Hi Matt, why are you here?" And I was like, "I want to, you know, observe the board meeting, see what you guys talk about, see who's on the board," and he said, "Well, you can't and you have to leave." And so, elected Public Hospital Commissioner was not allowed to observe the Board of the Association of Washington Public Hospital Districts, and I was like, who's on the Board? And he's like, "It's all CEOs," and I was like, "Well, can a Public Hospital Commissioner sit on the Board" and he said, "Oh no, it's in the bylaws that elected Hospital Commissioners cannot be on the Board of the Association that is basically the trade organization of all public hospital districts." I was like, "Well, that's interesting." And that also sort of opened my eyes to, these associations are controlled by CEOs basically, administrators. That means, they're never going to be controlled, even if I got all the public hospital commissioners to say they want to do something, they wouldn't have control over the organization. So that led to another tactic, which possibility of creating a different organization of network of public hospital commissioners potentially just going that route, just going around the obstacle. I haven't done that yet, but it's one of the things that we talk about in our group of 20.

Let's see what else we've got here. That was a dive into my political sort of journey. I might come back to the big picture of activism, the world. So I kind of consider my work in politics sort of like a hobby. What I really care about is trying to help alleviate oppression in the world. I believe we have a beautiful planet here, I believe there's enough resources for us to share the resources, so every human on earth should be able to live a reasonably thriving life, but the problem with our world is the power of pyramids. Every country basically has a power pyramid, 'cos every country has a type of hierarchy, whether it has a king, or a president, or a legislature, or an oligarchy at the top, or warlords, dictators, everyone fits into this power pyramid in some way, and it's very difficult to imagine how to disrupt that. I mean, human history is the story of power pyramids being created and eventually power being abused, and people being oppressed, and people at the bottom of the pyramid finally getting fed up and tearing the whole thing down, having a big revolution, and then, what happens? What happens after a revolution? Anyone know?

Students: [Unintelligible 01:03:15]

Matt Ready: I couldn't tell what anyone said.

Student 2: A restructure of the government.

Matt Ready: A new government. Some sort of new government is built. That's the way it's always been, and creates some sort of new power pyramid. And the cycle just repeats. But something has changed in the last, I would say 50 years, and it really was the internet. The internet has created a situation where the first time the vast majority of people in any country can be connected and communicate, and potentially, if we figure out how to do it, they could figure out how to use the internet as a way to control our collective power [unintelligible 00:04:07] communication to control our collective power. I actually believe this is the destiny of the internet and technology. It is going to help us create societies that are more egalitarian than anything we've ever seen before in human history, 'cos we could never do it before. We didn't have the internet, you had telegraph, you can't ask a million people to help you with the decision if your communication is so slow it takes a year to get any sort of response. But with the internet we could potentially ask a million people a question and get an answer in 10 minutes. So with the internet—and I'm going to take you on a little journey—this is how I see the evolution of the internet.

This is Usenet. The first big thing that really united, started to unite people and unite human knowledge was news groups, and bulletin board systems. Anyone ever used Usenet, news groups, you know what I'm talking about? They still exist, not really. Very popular among young folk. So as I mentioned earlier, Digg was one of the first sites to say, anyone can send in a link to anything and then you just vote it up, you would dig it, and then it would help percolate the better ideas, more popular ideas to the top. Then there's of course Bulletin Boards or Message Boards, and there's -- these are all text-based forms. Reddit is basically I think the biggest most significant text-based social form. And then in the last 10 years, video has really started to become something that is ubiquitous, something that is everywhere, that anyone with a smartphone now has the capability not only of recording a video, but of doing live video. I could pull out my phone right now, and I could go via YouTube or Facebook, and potentially the whole world could be watching. I bet there's probably enough, you could probably have 10 feeds going on right now if everyone pulled out their phones and started doing it. This changes the formula of how power and communication works, and it's changing revolution.

This from Occupy Wall Street, and this is different, this is something that people that squash revolutions and that -- this is going to change the formula of how revolution works, and already has. The Arab Spring, this is the Global Occupy Movement, but before the Global Occupy Movement it really started in the Arab Spring, and the thing that was different there was all of the video cameras that were going on. This is Tahrir Square, Egypt. There's two things, two really important things to know about from this picture. One is, these two guys they changed the whole course of history because they documented it and they collected -- they did live videos and they were networking online. This was an incredibly well documented revolution. The other things that really take away from this is, making change is about taking space. This is a central square, by occupying a central square in a society, you are saying, "My message is important." And so basically, the whole Egyptian revolution was about taking the Square, they didn't have to like fight wars, they didn't have to fight battles. There were some, but the battles were around the Square, because the government felt, and they were right, if the people were holding this Square and saying, something needed to change because people were so fed up, it was like a rallying point and brought people together. So many people did die in trying to hold this Square, but this was it, it was about this central space, and they could not, once the masses came, they could not stop revolution and the leader had to step down. Again, things have not gone all that great since then.

Now, these guys, they did all their documenting of this revolution and *The Square* is a movie that they put together, it's on Netflix, a really fascinating story, I strongly recommend.

Ukraine also had a very well documented revolution, which is still a pretty big mess, but that's another—*Winter on Fire*—another fascinating documentary, you'll learn a ton just absorbing the sort of front lines of what these people are going through. I watched these two movies, and you'll see so many similarities in Ukraine and Egypt, and what it feels like. It's like, people are the same everywhere, we all want a better world and we all want to try to make it a world where everyone can thrive. It's just hard to figure out how to do it.

So a couple of years after these, the Arab Spring, this happened. This is Hong Kong, and a movement erupted in Hong Kong for democracy. Anyone know what country is in charge of Hong Kong?

Student 1: China.

Matt Ready: That's true. China is in charge of Hong Kong, but Hong Kong is kind of like Puerto Rico is to the U.S. It is, I think it's called a protectorate. So it's not a part of mainland China, which is important. In any case, it is ultimately controlled by China, and when I saw that this democracy movement was erupting in China, it really caught my attention, and it really got me fired up because there's been democracy movements in China before. Anyone know when? Anyone know a major democracy movement in China in the last 40 years?

Student 3: That's a long time.

Matt Ready: Anyone know this picture?

Students: Yeah.

Matt Ready: Tiananmen Square 1989. There was a massive democracy movement in 89 and if you've watched documentaries about this, it was an amazing powerful populous movement centered again around a central spot, Tiananmen Square. They occupied the Square, students, college students, and then the only way that the powers in Beijing and China could squash it, they sent in tanks. My understanding is, they sent the tanks in and they told the soldiers and the generals, "We don't want anyone hurt," you know, because people were getting hurt and people were getting upset, "We don't want anyone hurt, but we want the Square cleared by the morning," giving sort of mixed signals, no one really knowing what they were telling them to do, and about 2000 people, they estimated, were killed. But this is one of the most, to me this is one of the most important images that you'll ever see in your life, because it shows you the incredible power of action. This was the day after 2000 people had been crushed, and tanks were just like doing a display and coming down this road, and this guy was carrying his groceries, just walked out there and stood in front of the tanks.

And again, this is what activism comes down to: where are you standing and why are you standing there? Because when you know what you're doing and why you're doing it, you can stop an army. The guy driving that tank, he didn't know why he was driving that tank down the road, he didn't know what he should do. He didn't want to kill anybody. I mean, this is like the most powerful act I've ever seen a human do. And he actually just got up on the tank [laughs], he got up on there and the tanks tried to go around him and he just -- I mean, that is the power of activism. That's why they went in, they crushed the occupied camps, they have to move you out of the power of spaces, and so if you know where the power is in your community, you can change anything, you go and you literally stand or sit for what you believe in. Now, of course, it was a powerful moment, no one really knows what happened to him afterwards. So, back to Hong Kong. Students had come out and they had actually stormed the government building. They just stormed it and overwhelmed it and they were sitting in it, and more students came out. The Hong Kong police were sent out and started pepper-spraying everyone and trying to get them to disperse. The students got umbrellas and raincoats and goggles and they stayed there. They held their ground. They weren't violent. So I was watching this and I was like, oh my gosh, I mean this is incredible, what's happening there? Don't know how this is going to go 'cos I'm thinking about Tiananmen Square, I'm like, when is China going to send in tanks? Here are just some images, people that were down there. And again, it was student-led, this is a teacher saying, "They [unintelligible 00:14:42] drama, I see students on the street, I get upset, I'm an adult, I need to come out and support and stand in front." So the students inspired many adults to go out, but it was mainly student led. So the pepper spray wasn't working, so you know the people that are in charge of Hong Kong, they called up Beijing and they said, pepper spray is not getting these students out of the streets. What do we do? They escalated to tear gas. That's never been done in Hong Kong before. The tear-gassed the students. Chaos and the students come back. Tear gas did not get them to leave.

Student 4: Better than being shot.

The Mindful Activist

Matt Ready: Yes. Well, see, that's what I'm sitting here thinking, they just escalated to tear gas and it didn't work, so what's going to happen next? Is it going to go to guns and tanks?

Student 3: Did they do like a [unintelligible 00:15:40] backgrounds or [unintelligible 00:15:42] bullet proof stuff, or they didn't go that far?

Matt Ready: I don't think they -- at this point they hadn't gone that far.

Student 4: [unintelligible 00:15:47] this is 2014, so what happened there?

Matt Ready: Yeah, we're getting there.

Student 4: All right.

[Laughter]

Matt Ready: So tear gas happened, and this is again, I want to go back to where I was, so I was sitting here just like watching this, and I'm like, oh my gosh, I'm going to sit here and we're going to see another Tiananmen square, we're going to see these students get slaughtered. So I was like, I want to help, I don't want to sit here and there's people actually getting, potentially they're going to get killed. So I was like, what can I do? I wanted to be active in this, I wanted to do something. I could start Facebooking it to support it, I could start blogging about it, I could maybe make some videos about it, I could send money or supplies --

[Background noise]

Matt Ready: So I tried to connect online with protesters. I did some of all this 'cos I feel that I could help. I just want to like, for those protesting, I was like, I can help you, I'm an activist organizer, I'm a very good tactical thinker, this is a big deal, I want to help you guys, but I wasn't satisfied with all this so, you know, I'm meditating -- this

The Mindful Activist

is what came up for me, I could go there. I didn't really know what I could do if I went there, but I was like --

Student 3: Arm the students.

Matt Ready: Arm them? Yeah, no.

Student 4: They have two arms already, they don't need more.

Matt Ready: You're not going to win all these fights, all these struggles with actual violence. But I decided to go there, so I went, I bought a ticket to Hong Kong and I just went to the protest sites. They took over the city these students, they blocked like four major areas, this is a highway, it's the equivalent of blocking I-5 in downtown Seattle, and they had tents, it was completely blocked, completely shut down, and this was, when I got there it had been shut down for like 10 days or 2 weeks already. This was the scene.

Student: Wow.

Matt Ready: They had taken these barricades, these are -- they'd blocked roads, and this was a government building they blocked, I mean they just swarmed the city, they had protest messages plastered all over the place and all sorts of interesting tactics going on. Universal Sufferage without civil nomination. They wouldn't let, I don't know if I actually said that point, did I explain what they were specifically protesting? They get to vote for their leader, but Beijing selects the candidates, so they're like, "this is pointless."

Student 4: I was going to say, that sounds familiar.

Matt Ready: Yes, it's kind of like the U.S. where corporations and corporate money chooses our candidates. But they were like fed up with it. Here are some images from some of the young people that led this. This was in a square, a very busy square they had taken over, and they were surrounded by very heavy claustrophobic business district, and they had a mic and people would get up and they would share the mic and they would say -- give their speeches

The Mindful Activist

and say what they had to say. And I was just sort of sitting bearing witness. I was like, if nothing else, I'm going to sit here with camera and I'm going to document, 'cos if the tanks do come, I'm going to at least be -- I didn't know what I would do actually, to be honest, I might have --

Student 5: RPGs.

Student 7: Can you shush?

Matt Ready: [Laughs] No, seriously. I mean, what do you do if someone is getting physically oppressed, or about to get, you know, about to get beat up by cops? If you're standing there, especially if you're in another country, but you're standing there and someone, like a student, is getting pressured by a line of cops, you know, it's like, what do you do?

Student 4: Why didn't you bring your tank to Honk Kong?

Student 5: Yea.

Matt Ready: [Laughs] I brought my camera, a camera is a powerful thing. And I think that's what stopped the tanks from going into Hong Kong, 'cos there were cameras everywhere. Anytime there's a slight confrontation you'd see like 50 cell phones come up and it was being filmed, or live-streamed. It created almost like a magic safety bubble. I mean, people did get beat up and hurt, but once they got beat up and hurt, they got photographed, and the pictures of people that got hurt and were bloody were just plastered all over the city. So it was like an instant shaming of the people using violence. I enjoyed taking pictures of the old Chinese men who would walk up, and I know people that lived through Tiananmen Square, who were there and alive, who you know are sitting there like, "Are you kids crazy? You know what China's going to do to you if you keep doing this." And they would just stop on the street, you know, coming down their way and they would just stare at it. I just found it, you know, sometimes you could see inspiration, you could see fear in their eyes.

I like this one. This is serious, like, I don't know what's going to happen in this scene now. There's a tactic, they put up this all over the plaster, all over the city again, this is a message straight to the police trying to tell them, "Don't use violence. You are committing an international crime if you use violence against these peaceful protesters." They put things like this, saying this is what the government is doing, this is what we're doing, they are hurting unarmed citizens, beating them with batons, using pepper spray, tear gas, threatening gun fire, colluding with Triad—that's a gang, organized crime in Hong Kong that there was a lot of evidence the government was actually paying thugs from the gangs to go and beat up protesters, just start fights, or sexually assault the young girls over there.

Student 4: Could you go back to the last slide? I was just wondering, do you happen to know what the Nuremberg principles are? I don't want you expand on everything, but I just never heard of it.

Matt Ready: I believe that's a reference to the rules of -- that came out of World War II, sort of, what the Nazis did; do we have some level of, even in war, of what is okay.

Student 4: I don't mean to keep you going back.

Student 3: Did the principles come out of the Nuremberg Trials that happened post World War II?

Matt Ready: Yes. I think you're onto something there [laughs].

Student 2: That's a good list.

Matt Ready: Yeah. That's a good one, because it's like a powerful reference they're using. It was weird while I was there, because there were a lot of young people, and the women, the young girls, the college girls and high school girls that were there, they also created a sort of safety bubble, because it's really hard for the police to come and beat up a bunch of students if there's, you know -- it's one thing to beat up a bunch of guys and have pictures of a guy's bloody nose, it's okay -- not okay, but it's easier for a society to stomach. But young girls getting hurt? It really -- I think it really prevented a lot of escalation of violence, and so what they tried to do, they tried to scare the girls away by threatening sexual assault. They actually had it said in the press, "We cannot keep girls safe, you should stay home," and they did. There were some instances of attempted sexual assault, but the protesters just said that, you know, if these are the tactics they're using, we're going to change our tactics of how we're going to keep people safe. And it just fascinated me how they took over this city, I mean, just blatantly challenging the Government Headquarters. What is a democracy? Democracy is the freedom to elect your own dictators.

Student 4: That's clever.

Student 5: Oh, man.

Matt Ready: So I met Lorie on the streets of Hong Kong during the protest. She grew up in Hong Kong until she was 12. She did the exact same thing I did. She was actually living in New York and when they started the teargas, she just bought a ticket and flew there. I interviewed her on my podcast, I'll tell you a little more about it. So, oh, this was going to be a question. Who's the highest ranking U.S. politician to visit Hong Kong Umbrella Movement protest sites?

Students: [Crosstalk]

Matt Ready: Hospital Commissioner, Matt Ready.

[Laughter]

Matt Ready: So then I come back to the hospital and an election comes up, and I decide to -- fortunately for me, a couple people are willing to run for office on the Hospital Board, and so there were a couple campaigns they went and they were -- I thought they would be stronger allies on the board and so I supported them both, and this

The Mindful Activist

guy actually won. So now I have another pretty strong voice on the board to work with me. Again, that's another tactic, and that's working within the system politics, you're in a political system, running candidates is a way to change the power dynamic.

Okay, so now we're going to get into my big strategy for how to fix the world, how to fix power in the world. It's about global consensus. It's about how do you bring the power of consensus decision-making, egalitarian decision-making to the whole world, so that millions or even billions of people can wield power together?

Student 4: Stop recording.

Matt Ready: Stop recording?

Student 4: I was joking.

[Laughter]

Matt Ready: So we need to be able to do this in a way that is fast, efficient and fun, has to scale to billions. I think it's basically the way social media is evolving, you know, Facebook -- the idea of Facebook is that it connects everyone, right? Connects billions of people, but we don't use Facebook as a tool for collective decision-making. But I think we could evolve social media into a tool for collective decision-making, and part of this, part of getting to that level, is leveraging full audio and video. Again, there's a problem on the internet with trolls, people are becoming trolls. Everyone know what I mean by a troll?

Students: Yes [crosstalk].

Student 4: No, no one knows [jokes].

Matt Ready: I think people are comfortable being so mean on the internet because of the anonymity. It sort of gives you this like barrier, and you just let your worst self out because no one knows it too. But there's no reason that we have to have collective platforms

The Mindful Activist

where there's that anonymity. You have platforms where you have to say who you are, and you have to show your face, or you have to say what you have to say out loud now. And so I think we leverage that, and again, it will sort of bring out a little bit of a better selves of people, and we can create the safer environments. So I've been working on this and thinking about this for a while, and the Global Consensus Project and Hive1 are the two websites where you can learn more about, and I'll show you a little bit with it. The idea is that we're basically sort of building a global hive mind, of human mind, or network of hive minds—and I like the hive metaphor 'cos it's better than the Borg metaphor—but my idea is that in a really functional human hive mind decision-making platform is totally egalitarian, no one is forced to pay attention to anything, no one is forced to listen to anything, no one's forced to stay silent or limit their expression, no one is forced in anyway. It's all volunteer participation, and it's safe. It's an environment that stimulates brainstorming, listening, speaking, exploring and expressing together. Basically, help us find answers together in more efficient ways.

Professor: Matt? I mean it might just be me, but is there anybody else that doesn't know what a hive mind or a Borg mind is? Anybody else? Everybody else knows but me?

Student 1: A hive is a [unintelligible 01:28:57].

[Laughter]

Professor: Oh, you do?

Matt Ready: Well, a hive is like a beehive, right? In a hive or an anthill, all these members of the hive are working together in some sort of team like way.

Professor: Oh, teamwork.

Matt Ready: Yeah. But the hive analogy breaks down a little bit because in a lot of hives there is a queen, so there is like a -- is that what you were going to say?

Student 3: Yes.

Matt Ready: So we're talking about something that we don't really have a metaphor for, a hive that is perfectly egalitarian. I might be wrong, there might be hives that don't have queens.

Student 5: You mentioned it like a [unintelligible 00:29:40] so is it like a -- so how do you, in the system, how do you [unintelligible 00:29:49].

Matt Ready: Right, well, I'm going to show you a little bit of it and we'll see how that does for us. Oh, 'cos I know this is a very hard concept to understand and so I have built the beginning of this platform, but I've started a podcast which is basically just -- because everyone knows what a podcast, or a webcast or a video show is, and so that is my vehicle for trying to introduce people to it. You just watch, anyone interested can start to watch the video webcast and we're going to interact with the Hive platform, and hopefully that'll be a way for people to start to understand how it can work and for me to understand how it can work, 'cos it's a very new idea.

These are just images from the podcast where I interview activists. Actually, I just interview people, but I ask everyone that I interview, "Are you an activist?" Just like I asked you guys. And we talk about different things. Okay, so now we're going to go a little bit into The Hive platform and we'll see if it makes any sense to you guys. So this is the main interface currently for the Hive platform, and it's basically designed to allow for egalitarian facilitation. I said that several times, it's how do you make -- how do you take a room full of people and make it so everyone is equal in making a decision, whether it's ordering a pizza or choosing whether or not we invade a country, or whatever. So one thing that has to has to happen is someone has to be able to facilitate the room, and so in this case I'm the facilitator, this person -- the facilitator has control over this,

The Mindful Activist

which is basically like a room in the Hive, and the facilitator can state a topic or a question here, and that becomes the focus of everyone that's in this room. And then anyone in the room can submit an answer and it comes up in this thread of answers, and anyone in the room can vote up or down any of these answers, and that sort of becomes one way that the Hive percolates up ideas. With me so far? [Laughs] That's not all that unusual for the internet, but each of these links, if you click on one of those, it becomes another room. So if you want to go and talk about theater activism, you click on that and now you're in a new room with a new facilitator and potentially all new information here. The facilitator also has the power to put up to four videos here, of information related to whatever this topic is. My vision of this is that it would be live. The middle video here would be a live person talking to people in this room. It could have thousands or millions of people in it. And again, anyone can participate, anyone in the room can express themselves in a couple different ways, you can answer the question, you can also do a sparkle up, sparkle down, or raise your hand. This came out of the Occupy movement, at least for me, it came out of the Occupy movement as a way of, you look at a room of people and you say, "Who likes Pizza?" You just go like this if you like pizza. Who likes ice cream? Yeah, so it's like a quick way. So who wants to end this meeting right now? You know, you can sparkle up, and when I'm facilitating, I'm constantly asking, how does everyone feel about extending this topic for 10 minutes? And you get a sparkle really quick, instant information from a group of people. A very powerful tool. Sparkle up, sparkle down, or sparkle straight out, it means I'm not sure. Anyone ever seen these before? Familiar with it?

Students: No.

Matt Ready: Very powerful tool. Also, in a lot of groups you can do this at any time, so it's not just when the facilitator asks you a question, or what are you going to do, anytime someone is talking, you can just go like this or go like this, and you're communicating in that moment how you feel about what's being said, but you're doing it in a way that is not oppressive to them as opposed to -- I mean even applause is a little bit oppressive because it stops the speaker

The Mindful Activist

from being able to speak when it gets too loud. And of course, yelling or whistling or hissing at someone is a way also.

Professor: So how hard it this to set up? I mean, is it something that people in this room --

Matt Ready: Yep.

Professor: -- could easily do? Would it be -- how would -- is anybody wondering that? That they would want to -- Jane, weren't you talking about doing something with the internet?

Student 8: An online quiz.

Matt Ready: Yeah, I mean, you could easily do an online quiz here with this, and yes, you guys could use this right now, so I'll just sort of take you through it. Let me go back to the beginning here. So these are the Genesis Nodes. It starts with -- basically there's like starter nodes for this Hive. So I have one for The Mindful Activist, and so that's one I control for my podcast and I put ideas in there, and you follow the threads of the ideas. I have right here, this is my first focus for the Mindful Activist, you can ask me any question, and these are some topics that are there, and if you're interested in one, you can go into it and you can put more links or answers, and each one can have -- each time you enter any sort of answer here you can associate a video, a YouTube video, by putting the YouTube video code right there, and it becomes the video that comes up when someone clicks on it. And then if you are creating the node, you can add other videos that you want over here. So, if you wanted to play with this, what you would do is you would go into the test node and you just, right here, where it says, "what test nodes exist for personal use" then you would just put whatever you want here, it could be the name of your first branch in this Hive Mind, it could be about anything, it could be your name. But then once you have it, once you go into it, you're going to be the facilitator immediately of the first node you create, so you can state whatever question you want, or statement here, you can invite people, you could answer the question

The Mindful Activist

here and invite people to vote on them, or you can invite people to give answers...

Professor: So who's the audience?

Matt Ready: It's whoever you invite to --

Professor: So you have to invite people into it.

Matt Ready: Well, yeah, until there's a community that's actually there, and you have to log in using Facebook. Facebook is the way you identify yourself to this as hopefully a semi-real person. Yeah?

Student 5: A lot of the problems that I see [unintelligible 00:38:02] and a lot of times like things are just not interesting and people are just not going to watch stuff like this, so I was wondering if you have [unintelligible 00:38:17] as to how [unintelligible 00:38:19] more interested in it.

Matt Ready: The youth? Did you say get the youth more interested?

Student 5: Yeah, [unintelligible 00:38:25].

Matt Ready: More interested in...?

Student 5: [unintelligible 00:38:29]

Matt Ready: Yeah, how to get people interested in -- I don't know, I don't really focus on -- I don't try to manipulate what people are interested in. I think the key to making positive change in the world is that you go to where you want to make the change, and where you want to make a difference, and what happens instead is people see you take action, and they are inspired by you, or they're affected by you, and you can invite them, I mean if you go -- like (a lot of activists are at?) Standing Rock and the fight over the oil pipeline in The Dakotas, so they're talking about it and they're doing events, they're organizing some sort of form or protest event, and they are networking and all you can really do is invite people, and then if

The Mindful Activist

they come, that's the next most important step. The next step is how you hold the space when you invite people in? If you invite people into a space and you want them to learn about something, you have to really decide how are you going to do that, are you going to invite them in and then just lecture them? Or are you going to invite them in and ask them questions and invite them to participate? There's a very big difference on how people respond.

Professor: So if I may say, so what you have is a team, so right now you already have a community of people that are interested in the same topic you are, and I think what Matt's saying is, you just need to do something, and then other people will join you or ask questions, do I --

Matt Ready: Yeah. I mean, action is what has an impact on the world, and if you do an action that is visible, it's going to impact everyone that sees it. That's the whole point of a direct action of some sort of event, or just going in to a square at the College Campus and just standing literally on a soapbox or anything, saying what you have to say, or creating a play or something and acting that out, or making a song, I mean, anything. Making art.

Professor: Or a graffiti --

Matt Ready: Or a graffiti.

Professor: -- or something. There's so much you could do just on this campus.

Matt Ready: And another part of it is to make sure you're being authentic and you're having fun, really like putting your heart in and trying to bring joy to the journey that you're on, 'cos you're pushing against the ocean here, trying to make change in the world, and so you want to be stirring up fun positive energy while you're doing it, 'cos there's going to be lots of times when it's really hard. All right, let's see here.

Professor: I'll just need maybe 6 minutes at the end.

Matt Ready: Yeah, and we were -- we stop at 3:15? Is that the...?

Professor: Yeah, 3:14 [laughs].

Matt Ready: Well, that's basically, other than like trying to explain more of how the Hive works, that's basically my stuff. I've got a lot of video on the Hive (?) about different aspects of what I'm doing and since it's there, I'll show you one more piece of it. So one thing that I've sort of been using it for is, it's a great way to organize your own ideas and then be able to instantly attach videos to the ideas. You can quickly go back and sort of be like, oh, that was interesting, and stick a video next to it, 'cos every time you put a link in, if you put a video in, it becomes more meaningful for you and more informative, and as you keep going with that -- so basically, each of these ideas sort of builds on the next one, and so each video then becomes sort of the thread to the idea, and so it becomes in a way, a video blog. I'm just going to keep going into this 'cos I want to show you -- so I've been clicking through ideas, each one that connects -- and this is a documentary about the work, basically about me and the work I'm doing, sort of stitching these clips together, here up to the first words I say in the hospital boardroom, this is on the first debates, okay.

So you might not have gotten the full sense of that you just threaded through like 10 videos there. If you're watching you could but what this little guy here, that little arrow, it actually changes the interface, so this is a much faster interface for cruising through the Hive and what you're looking at now is the thread you just followed of ideas and videos stacked on top of each other. So if you say, if you were researching some activist topic or any topic you're interested, and you did this, you could basically use this link to be a way to share with someone or just for yourself to share, basically a video blog, like a mini -- it's almost like creating a little documentary that way. Does that make any sense? And that's probably what the way this is going to go. It's going to be -- and to get back to the Hive, the main interface, there's just this little Hive link and it takes you back into the main interface. And this is just the beginning, this is what I was able to build my level of expertise. But basically what I'm doing is

The Mindful Activist

I'm trying to, as I share this with people and talk about it, I am looking to build up sort of a development community to help sort of make this -- to help improve this and make it really user-friendly, 'cos right now it's at the very, it might not be the most user-friendly interface at the moment.

Okay, if you want to learn more or just follow what I'm doing, or use the software, then http://hive1.net is the place where you can actually use that Hive platform. Again, you just go into the test node and create your own, or just go in and start messing around, answer questions and play with it, and you'll get the hang of it that way. These other websites are the other ways to follow what I'm doing. This is my actual Hospital Commissioner Website, and then I'm on Facebook and Twitter.

Professor: Can you have that on my desktop right now and I'll have a copy of this modified down a little bit so that they can have some of the information of what you just presented?

Matt Ready: Yeah, you can have the whole presentation and do whatever you want with it.

Professor: Okay, so I'll put this up on Campus for those who'd like to take a look at these connections.

Matt Ready: So that's basically what I've got for you today. Do you want them to break into their teams briefly?

Professor: They're in their teams now. Do you have some questions for Matt, ideas that may be came to you. I asked you to write down at least three that he could give you some more details about or help answer any questions you may have?

Student 1: I know I've been asking a lot of questions, but I promise I've been saving this one for the whole presentation.

Matt Ready: All right.

Student 1: You say like this is mindful activism, so when you were first starting the present -- I'm not trying to step on your toes, I promise.

Matt Ready: No, go for it.

Student 1: When you were talking about like protesting like at Bank of America and making sure people can't get it, and then I sort of saw that as mindless activism, until you started going into about what you do with the hospital and even with the Hive Mind. Would you agree or disagree with me that your activism improved or do you think that they're both were just activism?

Matt Ready: That's interesting. I did say we were blocking the entrance, we did obstruct the entrance, but we did not -- I was not comfortable and some activists totally would block the entrance, so we did not do that and I was not willing to do that. I was comfortable just obstructing and then, you know, a few people did go by us. And so I still feel that I was being very thoughtful about what I did and what I was willing to do there. But it was definitely -- I hope I've improved, it's definitely a learning experience. And I was, back in Occupy, I wasn't sure about the tactic of going after Bank of America. I wasn't really sure that was the greatest tactic, but everyone thought it was good and I thought all right, I'll put my brain and my efforts into this 'cos it seems everyone thinks this is a good way to attack corporate power, and so I just thought I'd just give it a try.

Student 1: I mean, I applaud you for trying, like I said, I don't want to step on your toes 'cos that's still a good thing.

Matt Ready: You're not stepping on my toes.

Student 7: So that's like who you were trying to reach by setting up those tents, you were trying to get like recognized by Bank of America? Like what were you trying to call?

The Mindful Activist

Matt Ready: Well, for me it was a -- you know, we had just bailed out the banks, it was just sort of like a blatant use of the government and taxpayer money to help private corporations, so I was calling attention to that. And for me it was basically calling attention to every one of the gross abuses of corporate power there is. They were saying the banks were too big to fail and we're basically saying they were too big to exist, they weren't doing us any good. And so it was just trying to get everyone's attention. Did that answer your question?

Student 7: Yeah. I have another one.

Matt Ready: You have another one?

Student 7: So like did you guys inform the people like that walked by you to go into the bank or did you just try to obstruct?

Matt Ready: Oh no, there were protest signs, they were one way to get your basic message out, and we had we had like a play, and we had singers, and yeah, I mean the dialogue that happens around an activist action is kind of like the most important thing that's going on, 'cos that's where you're really stimulating debate and questions.

Student 5: I was wondering like, what's your philosophy when trying to fix the problem [unintelligible 00:50:57].

Matt Ready: Yeah, I mean the Hive platform is my strategy. I think we just need to sort of teach each other that the people in the country actually have all the power, if we just learn how to actually use it together. And the tactic used to stop us from doing that is to prevent us from uniting and talking about it, and so the tactic they try to divide us by coming up with issues that will divide us, and even they try to divide the left-wing and right-wing to keep them from uniting and really just seeing. All we have to decide is what we want, 'cos once enough people even in a state just say, we want this, it becomes really hard for the state legislators to say no. If we have everyone in the state saying we want state-based single-payer healthcare, or whatever, it's really, really hard to just ignore that once it's clearly stated by the people. It becomes very transparent, the corruption becomes very transparent. There's another question back there?

Student 3: So our [unintelligible 00:52:21] is on the mentally ill homeless, and basically what our idea was, was to raise awareness for politicians that blame millennials are concerned with this issue basically. Off the top of your head, what would be like a good first step for us to do, in order to do that?

Matt Ready: So the mentally ill and homeless.

Student 3: [unintelligible 00:52:43]

Matt Ready: And your tactic is to get the politicians to care about it, that's you trying to get into.

Student 3: Well just show them that there's public interest in that social issue.

Matt Ready: Yeah. I would -- it's good to sort of have a specific action that you want the politician to do, that you can really sort of like pressure them with that. So if you have some idea of like if there's a facility that needs to be expanded, or if there is -- if you find an innovative program somewhere in the country that's doing something really great for the mentally ill and homeless, you can say, "Why don't you do that? Why don't you replicate what was done in this area? Or you just come up with your own idea, like we need more outpatient Mental Health Services or we need more inpatient Mental Health Services. Yeah. I mean [unintelligible 00:53:39] you know. And you might want to talk to people that are like really, really engaged in that issue 'cos they'll have -- when you find someone that's engaged, they'll have ideas, they'll be like, this is what we need, and they'd love to see some people go and fight and pressure for these solutions that they've come up with.

Student 5: In your early days of networking, how much networking did you do on social media?

The Mindful Activist

Matt Ready: In my early days of networking? You mean for like – I mean, I have been on the internet since the internet explosion, so I have like a lot of history on the internet, but in the early days it was socializing. Now it's become -- now it's part of my political and activist work. I don't know what you're getting out of that question.

[Laughter]

Student 5: I'm just asking like how much did you do and how like it affected what you're trying to reach people to do.

Matt Ready: You know, actually I find networking online to be the worst kind of networking. The best kind is going to a meeting, like just find people that are doing something related to what you want to network about and go in person. When you're in person with someone, it's so much more powerful than online, but what it does it feeds your online presence. If you go to a meet up for something, and you speak up and you say, hey, I'm doing this or I'm trying to raise awareness on this mental health homeless person issue, and you say it, you'll go home and you'll have like 10 people just followed you on Twitter from that meet up. They've seen you and they know you. When I went to the Occupy National Gathering it was crazy, 'cos I was suddenly meeting all these people, and suddenly my phone was blowing up while I'm at the National Gathering from people I'm meeting there, they're immediately following me on their phone, and it was the most successful online networking I ever did because I was in person actually meeting real people. Yes?

Student 4: I just wanted to [unintelligible 01:55:44].

Matt Ready: I do, and I have a bunch of cards here, so I'll put some out and anyone that wants one can have one. It has my contact info on it, and really, you guys are welcome to contact me if you ever want feedback on anything related to activism or meditation, really. So that offer's out there until I get to complain by saying I get too many contacts.

[Laughter]

The Mindful Activist

Matt Ready: Then I'll have to change that. But then I'll use the Hive. I'll still have that *ask me anything*, so you can just ask a question there, there's thousands of people.

Student 2: You talked a lot about how like, being like a politician and trying to change things, was a lot about like carefully picking your tactics. Like currently a large issue is like the Senate like blocking the selection of the new Supreme Court Justice, and even though your like important tactics was like making it transparent, it's like the public, like everyone knows, it's very obvious what they're doing and nothing's being done.

[Recording ends]